RESONATING AFFIRMATIONS

THE DECLARATIONS REQUIRED TO MANIFEST DESIRES

RINZEN JOYE

OMNIPION
PUBLISHING

RinzenJoye
Copyright page

Publisher: Omnipion Publishing

For permissions contact: Omnipion Publishing PoBox 240
SANDBACH CW11 5EA

Edition: 1st

ISBN paperback: 978-1-911655-01-5

Edited by: Omnipion Publishing

Cover Design by Julian Roberts at Omnipion Publishing

"Handle them carefully, for words have more power than atom bombs."

    -Pearl Strachan Hurd-

Resonating Affirmations has been given a 5 star seal of approval from Readers' favorite! Here's what they had to say...

Reviewed By K.C. Finn for Readers' Favorite...

Resonating Affirmations: The Declarations Required To Manifest Desires is a work of self-help non-fiction penned by author Rinzen Joye. After a deep and personal journey through a variety of self-help media herself, the author has developed an amalgamation of popular beliefs and practices with which she has had personal success, marrying them to her own spiritual and scientific philosophies to create a powerful attitude to life improvement, and a deeper connection with the universe around us. In a similar style to the theory of the Laws of Attraction, Rinzen Joye asks her readers to join her in her own Resonation Realm, where 49 different affirmations will guide them to a better sense of self and how to achieve the success they dream of in life.

Author Rinzen Joye has created a more accessible version of the affirmation techniques than most authors, even offering a very helpful section on the nature of affirmation itself and its potential effectiveness from a variety of critical angles. I very much enjoyed her take on belief and trust, and how those things are built up over time. The affirmations also rhyme, which I thought was a truly excellent touch, because it makes the ones that really 'resonate' with you stick in your memory, and you can take them out into your daily life without needing the book to hand. Overall, Resonating Affirmations: The Declarations Required To Manifest Desires would be an excellent starter book for anyone wanting to include more positivity in their lives as a basis for change.

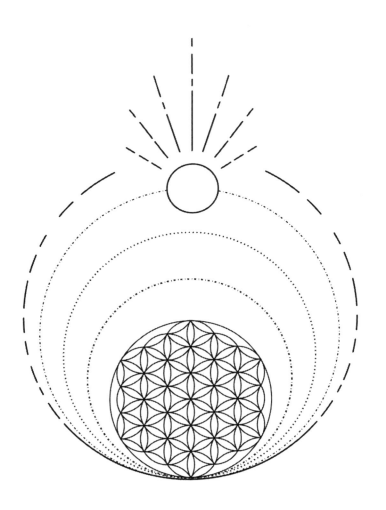

DISCLAIMER

Before you read this book, or any of the books in the Resonation Realm series, and take any of the advice from my teachings, I must point out that everything you are about to read is just my opinion. In my free book, Resonating System I shared with you my revelations, discoveries, and how I came to join the dots with spiritual teachings, scientific theories and philosophical views. I explain that my "bridging the gap" method that I feel gives us a "theory of everything that includes divinity and proves we have supermundane abilities" is just a concept (not a scientifically proven fact that I'm claiming exists) that I feel works to deepen my spirituality and allows me to be the spirit in skin I came to this planet to be. Therefore, you should only take my advice, adopt my philosophy, and use the supermundane tools for aligning your system to tap into the Mystical Zones that I teach in this book if you feel there's enough truth in what I say inside your soul to make up your own mind.

〜

I can advocate that the mindset and emotional state I suggest you need to succeed will be the most beneficial state to create your desires, but it still needs to be your logic that concludes whether what I say feels right to you, before any of my tools work for you. You may have resonated with my mission after reading my manifesto, or seen me online and already feel my books will work for you, but if you haven't done so already, I suggest you read my free book, Resonating System, first, so you're familiar with the terminologies I use throughout the series and as a guide to what I have to offer which will be of most value to you.

I don't want anyone to believe anything blindly, even if I know my views, skills and tools will work better than anything else on the planet for aligning you with the mystical powers of this cosmos. What I teach is what's true to me and, even though it has worked for others, I could well be a pathological nut job that is gullible enough to believe in her experiences so much that the placebo effect is proving her right big style!

∾

The fact is, if anything I say doesn't ring true to you, then it's not your truth and you should find a different path. All teachings are just a finger pointing to the moon, as the Buddha would say. Any of them can get you to see IT (Intelligent Transcendence) in your own way, feel IT in your own way, and have IT work for you as, no matter what you call IT, you will call upon IT, and IT will gift you the benefits that the Prime Mystical Zones impart on us.

I aim to speak to your heart, which is ultimately what works for most people but I must be clear in stating that, even if you fully trust enough to take everything I say on board, and you think you've done everything I suggest, for a rare few, the things you want, you may not be able to make happen in you life.

Why?

Because some people just need just one of my books in the series to totally get IT, and they're good to go, using the Mystical Zones with ease, others need the full series (which I suggest even if you're good to go because why not be invincible?) A rare few also need more practice in creating their dreams than others. Conjuring positive thoughtlings (thoughts and feelings together) takes a bright, booming, aligned heart and a clear, focused mind so you create the fully functioning avatar you need to push your "ask" past the frequency fields, into the Mystical Zones, but you also need to know how to take note of the intrinsic gut inclines and lightbulb moments (the instructions we need to take heed of from the Mystical Zones) we receive! Struggling to understand what the Mystical Zones are guiding us towards doesn't mean you are faulty or weak. Those who have been through a lot have plenty to undo but they have also learned more than others and are "winning the game" and "passing the test" more than they know. Those who still feel under years of significant "darkening attempts" that they are still connected to light, just need to get more determined to clear their system so they can perceive the signals from their stifled spirit once more!

I've had to scratch the old CD playing in my brain many times and rewrite myself a new tune to play on repeat. I've had to rip up roots buried so deep I thought I was pulling up my internal organs along with them as I tried to lift my repressed soul. There are still little offshoots of these dark, insistent branches inside me, trying to send my spirit back into the darkness but, each time they rear their ugly heads, I blast them away, treating them like a flash of memory, one that (after gaining composure) reminds me of how far I've come. I breathe through them, thankful I'm not a person who has to react towards the things that trigger these hindering thoughts and feelings anymore, so most just get bored and die, allowing my new, positive response to become habitual.

The key is to be kind to yourself. Just know that we must work all empowering information into our own belief system and life situations in our own time. It doesn't matter if it takes one read or ten for a new concept to sink in. If it takes counselling from a trained professional to get rid of unresolved psychological scars, or a shaman to banish those unknown energy blockages first, you're still heading in the right direction.

~

Bottom line, you should always come to your own conclusion upon discovering things like this along your path. I'm sure my tools will work for you as they do for me, and will help you create a wonderful life, but if you find that using them isn't for you, then you've at least learned what doesn't work and can eliminate it from your life once and for all. When we find things that don't work, it leads us to things that do. No matter the outcome, your path led you to this book for a reason. So take all the advice, take some, or throw it in the bin and take none. You can still use it as another stepping stone in your discovery of what works and what doesn't work best for you and hence be wiser by the end of this book because of it.

I think of my path like this: I have one backpack to accompany me on my journey, and I'm only allowed to put into it the things I know will benefit me. I carry all the best parts of the more peaceful religions, and teachings from a variety of profits and philosophers, my Reiki principles and techniques, and the unique resonating meditation, mantra and affirmation techniques that I invented through downloading divine information of my own, one of which you're about to learn in this book. When I'm not working towards goals in line with my spiritual intent, I do things that aid in my relaxation, joy, peace and happiness.

When my body needs me to rest, but my brain still needs to know I've worked towards my goals, I'll have bubble baths but watch things on YouTube that help my spiritual development, I'll paint but will listen to the kinds of music I want to create for inspiration, and will even watch anything that's fantasy and science fiction on Netflix because I can class the time as "research" since I'm writing (in the pen name of Debbie Zain), my own urban fantasy series I hope to sell to that network at a later date.

Anything I gather and put in my bag, and anything I do for pleasure, benefits me. As I am an ever-evolving being, some things stay, and some things don't. As long as I keep learning and forgiving myself for my mistakes along the way, I'm okay.

So see if this tool works for you, contemplate my philosophy and musings on what's out there in the universe and higher dimensions. If my resonating views bring a clearer understanding of the esoteric, mystical incomprehensible stuff that's above, and my tools create peace, joy, positivity, a sense of wellbeing below, allowing alignment with the powers that be like never before, then put them in your backpack! If my tools don't reprogram your brain to have beneficial beliefs, or clear the fear inside your heart, and lift your spirit, granting you access to the Mystical Zones on autopilot, and enabling you to create the life of your dreams with greater ease like I know they can, then leave them be. You only have room for what works best.

I'm 100% confident the strategies I teach are better than anything else out there. My resonating spin on the tried and trusted methods of many religions and spiritual practices will make more sense to people than all philosophies combined because I trust when we understand things instead of blindly believing them; we are more likely to include them in our daily lives, which means, because of my simplifying ways, along with my views, methods and tools, I will enhance your chances of success... but I still have to disclaim that this is just my belief, not a guarantee.

One statement the Buddha made that always resonated with me about his teachings was that we should not go by reports, legends, traditions, scripture, logical conjecture, inference, analogies, agreement through pondering views, probability, or thought; it's contemplating which is our teacher! When you know for yourself that these qualities are skilful, blameless, praised by the wise, or these qualities, when adopted and carried out, lead to welfare and happiness, then you should enter and remain in them.

I'm asking you to do the same.

FINDING AFFIRMATIONS

s far back as I can remember, I've felt that I came to this planet from some creative realm beyond the dimensions I'm bound to on Earth as a "creative uplifter of souls", and that I would one day express the gifts bestowed upon me from this mystical realm to the masses. I was so small when this artistic desire to entertain, act, sing, dance and paint manifested in me I used to say I want to be "in" the TV, not "on" it, thinking I had to transform into a miniature sized human to fit inside the box (which TV's looked like back then). This desire remained within me as I grew, and remains to this day, but the blissful, beautified version of my initial intent in its pure form has gone. I mean, the divine incline that fills me with excited awe at the thought of creating great art for people remains, but that idea I'd become a well revered star for adding so much joy and entertainment to millions of people across the globe tarnished.

Why?

Mainly, it's because of my brain adopting the fear-based warnings from highly opinionated people with self-limiting mindsets who spouted negative "truths" with no qualms in their attempts to save me from the pain, rejection, and failure that comes with the territory of being a creative individual. It's also because of the dream-squashing, darkeners of light-filled beings whose hatred programmed me with the self doubt that hindered my entire system. There could've been plenty of things in the last 30 years that all the jealous, spiteful people who killed the innocent, vibrant part of me back would've loved, if they'd have left me alone to be who I came to this planet to be. Instead, they made sure they attached the worry of all the things that could go wrong to the desire of my soul each time it reminded me of what it came to this planet to do.

The logical part of my mind told me to just focus on the good side of becoming an enormous success, but my heart knew better than to trust my logic. Hurt too many times before, my heart saw fit to cut off my ability to tap into the Algorithmic Zone, the mystical place that would've let me download the quickest path towards manifesting my desire. Because my heart wouldn't boom out my intent, I had to become my guide... a hard thing to do when the fear in your persona is louder than the desire of your psyche, which it was back then.

I'd been able to get into the Visionary Zone for years before the naysayers took effect. Creativity was always on my mind and therefore whenever I felt happy or relaxed I created the perfect Resonation Realm to enter the Visionary Zone, which gave me many lightbulb moments, inspiration and ideas. I could also gain access if I controlled my fear by telling myself I'd only use an idea I was tapping in to get once I had counselling or read more self-help books to help me deal with the success. I knew the muses of the zone wouldn't grant me the greatest ideas they had until I no longer feared becoming famous. When I tapped in to ask for the support I needed to write "the best urban fantasy series ever" I promised I would do my best with whatever inspiration the mystical story muse sent my way and meant it.

They didn't disappoint. That it took fourteen years before being happy to release this "Supermundane" series after the direction I received for them is another matter. Long story short, it was a never ending editing, honing, polishing and changing of the rules inside the magical systems and world of Omnipion. The entire era was one major pathological procrastination technique I adopted to save me from the "pain" I believed would come when releasing them because of my programming.

When I look back at my naïve, younger self, always making my friends sing songs I'd made up or act out shows I'd scripted in front of the whole street, never once lacking confidence, I feel like jumping into my vision and wrapping myself in a protection bubble. The conviction I had that I would one day make my dreams come true was due to not one person contradicting me, therefore my alignment in heart and brain (as well as my psyche) to become "famous" was a thing I presumed possible, until I was told otherwise... by almost everyone around me.

Most care givers must've viewed my intent to be "famous" as a childish dream that would pass when I got my list of "options" in school (none of which included drama). Back then, career advisors disregarded the arts as a "proper" career. If only I could go back and convince myself that I could have the desire of my soul with enough determination. I would've explained that care givers only wanted to protect me from the pain of rejection and their warnings of all the ways it might go wrong meant I only needed to work harder on my art to convince them. I mean, why can't people let people be who they should be? Help them by saying "if you want to go for it, then you must go for it"? Encourage them to do all they can to become the best at what they want? Instead, I was told "I would most likely fail" with a raised eyebrow that suggested I was deluded to even think I may make it.

I mean, I was already under the impression "I wasn't pretty enough to be an actress" from the bullies at school, bringing to my attention the fact that "I was spotty, ugly and unwanted". To give it its due, my self doubt wrestled with the idea that ugly people got roles too, and there would've been a place for my acting skills in some ugly role somewhere, but I felt then being ugly was so "wrong" it wasn't something I wanted to embrace. I'd equated ugly to being unworthy, a belief reinforced by the amount of rejection I'd already encountered because of it so I would've been ashamed when going for ugly roles.

No matter what my soul called for me to be, and how much I knew I should ignore my neurological conditioning, and trust I could live out its desire, the bullying and rejection I encountered as a child built an iron cage around my heart, which sabotaged every attempt I made to succeed. I couldn't even sing well enough at this point because of my mother shouting up the stairs that I sounded like a cat each time I practiced. My soul cried for me to push past those vocal barriers, my brain told me to consider my strengths and weaknesses so I could sing in keys I could reach without squealing, but the dichotomy within my system, caused by my stubborn heart, wouldn't grant me access to the Algorithmic Zone to send me the "how" for these ideas. My fearful heart and negative brain set about killing every dream my soul had.

If it wasn't for my one true friend (and the only other individual in my world who wanted to be a singer, who's still my bestie today) grabbing me by the back of the neck and shoving my face towards the mirror yelling "tell yourself you're beautiful now", I wouldn't have bothered reading every self-help book going, ones that gave me a newfound trust in myself, nor would I have found the spiritual teachings that allowed for me to understand others.

Her actions didn't make me think I was beautiful; but knowing someone (especially someone I looked up to and cared about who I dreamed statistically gorgeous and who never got picked on) wanted me to believe it helped. For the one human I truly cared for to get so annoyed with the negativity I was showing towards myself that they needed to grab me to make me see myself like they did was the only positive dichotomy my system that kept the tiny spark in my soul alive.

I didn't know about affirmations at the time (and I'm not sure my friend did either), but I knew I had to reprogram my brain with beliefs that supported my dreams. And I got what she was trying to do, but what she was trying to make me say was so alien to me, it was impossible for it to come out of my mouth; I couldn't even look at myself, let alone say something I utterly didn't believe. I didn't get that there was some mystical power to affirmations if you repeated them enough times, or their ability to override the false, limiting beliefs until years later. Her passionate intent to make me see what she saw made me view myself from her perspective, and ask myself how I'd act if I witnessed her spirit disintegrating in front of me. How would I feel if her fabulous, exuberant, confident nature vanished, and she walked beside me with her head hung low and a sad smile, frightened of the world, her beautiful soul squashed underneath the sh*t she'd allowed into her system? I wouldn't have let some shadow version like that take over her, that's for sure, a version that would've been a far cry from the potential she'd once set for herself.

The act made me see I had to act like I was my best friend, but talking to myself in the mirror, shouting something that was untrue, wouldn't work. I may have been beautiful on the inside, but I would never trust that the greasy, spotty girl looking back at me was beautiful. I got called a witch so many times because of my pointed chin I felt it was my duty to shrivel into a cackling melted mess like the wicked one in The Wizard of Oz. In an alternate universe, there's a version of me who took this weakness as a strength and starred in the Harry Potter films because of it, but the problem wasn't just embracing who and what I was and figuring out how that would serve me. After all the self-help books, I realised I wouldn't handle being "famous" because of all the negative aspects I then believed (because of my own perceptions) came with the role.

For example, growing up, my mum would shout at the TV when she saw a famous person she hated; this sent the fear to my heart that if I became famous, strangers would hate me for reasons I couldn't even control. I fixated my mindset on the fact that if I'm famous lots of people will hate me! She was also dead set against the rich, who were all, in her opinion, evil and corrupt. Also, back in my "I'm so ugly because people told me so" days, I couldn't stand having my photo taken. Thinking people may want to interview me sent my heart into a frenzy; mulling over the matter that I'd have to act false in order not to come across like the daft idiot I am and make a fool of myself, for one. I've always seen through people who act fake, never resonating with them, so I could not be something I wouldn't respect.

My brain conjured up many false beliefs and irrational worries each time I'd take one step towards an artistic goal because, by this point, I feared success and failure. I used to sit and wonder "how am I ever supposed to succeed when I'm so empathic"? And I'm glad for this kind of questioning because asking myself this question created the first thoughtling my heart didn't fear which gave me my first lightbulb moment from the Algorithmic Zone in years.

I could be creative and hide from the public eye, if I was just a songwriter!

That's when I took the rock songs I intended to sing after years of self-help to the singer in the band my friend drummed in, who was thankful for them. The day I heard him sing one on stage was the first time in years I'd felt whole. I'd heard that saying plenty of times but never really knew what it meant until then, as my soul cried happy tears throughout my entire body, sending a divine "that's what we're here for" shiver of euphoria down my spine. The worries of my persona vanished in that moment, obliterated by my booming, satisfied, radiant soul, determined once again I was here for more, and my ego couldn't deny this moment proved it could live out its true purpose, if I was resourceful enough.

I'd already been working on extracting the false beliefs about the situation, but the "truths" were harder for me to ignore or override.

I then asked myself, "how could I handle the nasty people hating me, slating me, trying to hurt and upset me?"

My go to lightbulb was "I'd do it despite them, prove them wrong, so it would teach them"... but I knew this kind of attitude wouldn't last long term. For one, it didn't sit well with the empathic nature of my soul, and two, my body wouldn't appreciate being permanently on guard, waiting for a fight. The revengeful thought process only made me harder and more argumentative than I was already becoming. I didn't want the loudmouth delinquent I portrayed (because of feeling it was my duty to take down every hater in it) to take over me neither.

I know my conscious brain feels that if I concentrate and dwell on the bad, then it will somehow help me prepare for it. It's logical if I can also see myself handling the unpleasant situation, no problem, trust myself and move on. I don't have to continue thinking of the bad associated with the good until it causes the associated negative emotions, causing my heart to protect me from the thing I actually want because of the fear I've then attached to it. I could simply understand there are hateful people out there criticising others, and it's more about them than about me. I don't have to know why or change myself; I just have to change my response to it and that's it!

What an epiphany!

I love the saying, "If you're not both loved and hated, then you're not anything".

Abraham Lincoln said, "You can't please all the people all of the time," and it's so true. Some of my most admired and favourite people get slated.

I knew it was the nature of the industry, but my heart had to be in on the logic for it to believe my mind. If there's any doubt, the feeling associated with the thought won't dissolve the fear. No matter how many self-help books you read to give yourself new thoughtlings, you can't fool your heart. What a complex system we have! As long as we know what's going on, recognise the emotion for what it is, and remain aware of the belief causing it, we can override the fear. And not just by "thinking positive". This doesn't work, especially when everything around you is falling apart and you feel you're on an ever-increasing downward spiral but it is, I'm sure, one reason we have an imagination. We are all creative. We can remember past times when we felt good. If not, we can imagine how good it would be to have the thing we desire and only the desire, not the negative connotations, or we can at least see ourselves handling the negative connotations with ease, if not.

My eldest son helped me too, as he usually does with his brilliant mind. He said, "fame is just a word, an inevitability of success. It is neither good nor bad, it just is, and it's just a word."

From my son's point of view, fame is just a consequence of success and hard work and dedication, nothing to feel proud of and nothing to fear, it just is. It's the emotion you have that makes a word become something more than it is; and you can change that. I can create my idea of fame.

Once I knew and understood all this, the conflict inside me shifted. I now understand that when I'm in my happy, visualising land, and imagine my novels making it big and a filmmaker wanting to make use of them, I should only feel the bliss of it. One positive thing about the fame game if I end up with any of the bad, is that I'll at least be able to afford the counselling!

If some people find my novels entertaining, my

spiritual books helpful, and my art healing or uplifting, then I've done something right. If I simply concentrate on self-worth, self-value, and self-love and keep talking to myself like I am my best friend, telling my heart there's no need to fear if I go for what my soul wants, that it can handle anything, including becoming successful, I'll be fine. People like to be critics, simple as! They don't need to understand how much time and effort I've put into my art to get it as good as it can be as they stab their finger into the one star rating they love to give those that have at least trued to entertain them. Or take into consideration that I chose not to go on holiday for ten years so I could afford to take every course out there so I could ensure they had the best experience when reading the novels I produce for them.

Dream squashers don't have to bother me! I have a good, charitable heart that would make such a lovely difference in the world if given a position of power, and kind, decent, wise people who know and see the real me will always wish me well.

Is this my answer to the question "how can I still live my dream, handle the haters, and be an empathic, loving being?"

Almost.

This answer came after I learned the psychology of

bullies being cowards. I asked my soul what it thought about haters and the answer came as "all souls are naturally happy, loving and kind and would never ordinarily hurt another soul". This made me look at the haters as humans that were more messed up than me, that they were beautiful souls scared inside damaged avatars, the perspective that sits well with my true nature because it's here to help all suffering beings, including theirs.

What perspective?

"I will be creative for the haters, not despite them".

I like Missy Elliot's line in one of her songs 'I'm least hated by the haters!' She says it like she is so proud that just a few hate her. It just goes to show what having a great perspective can do.

This helped me practice a light-hearted feeling towards what I once feared would come and gave me a way of knowing that I would be fine if that situation arrived. It also helped me concentrate on the preferable thoughtling that most people on the planet are kind and supportive and wish people well. I could do anything I feared because the fears that come true will be so few that they won't matter and, if they did, I can change my view.

It's my duty as a radiant being of light to not let "darkeners" win, not make this soul of mine dim. I shall continue being me until I win them over as I'm doing it for their soul, the one screaming underneath the hate inside them at me to ignore their messed up persona and continue!

Our souls need humans to be who they came here to be so we can, as a collective, know that no matter what we've been through, we can come through! If we're not someone's cup of tea, we may be their inspiration. We can let the world know that hate doesn't work, so haters can deem their attempts to stop others being who they came to be as futile. Maybe they need us to continue through their hate, so it reduces their own fear enough to be who they came to be. By having the spiritual perspective to see dark, hate filled, toxic individuals as suffering souls, filling our hearts with compassion, we make the world a better place.

THE SUBTLE TOOL

*I*f I'm going to use a tool, and feel it's the right thing for me to do, I usually need proof that it works. The reason I began using affirmations was when I found evidence that they could reprogram the negative thoughts we have on autopilot with positive ones, as that's what causes the positive emotions we need for our hearts to open and boom. Knowing we can override old neurological pathways that hinder our success with new beneficial ones that create clear thoughtlings was one thing, but knowing they have the power to reboot the whole system, leaving us with the balance we need to ease our way into the Vitality Zone where we can regenerate, relieve stress, depression, anxiety and pain was another. I had no fear in my heart about being well, allowing the energy to heal my body, but it also brought me back to a place where I could perceive the true inner voice of my authentic self once more. The being deep within who is always full of peace, harmony, understanding, kindness, compassion, forgiveness and appreciative, energised joy who could enter the higher dimensions on auto pilot.

How do they work?

Because the affirmation registers in our brains so much that our minds consider it to be true. Once the words become a part of our belief system, feelings follow, and this shapes how we view ourselves and the world. What I struggled with most when I first used affirmations, despite realising their potential power, was not believing the words I was saying, so they never had that much of an effect on me. I understood how when positive statements got repeated by others that they ended up creating the healthy, mental environment that causes a raise in their vibration, but I could never fool my heart.

My heart having a mind of its own, picking what it wanted to believe, frustrated me, especially when it would so easily react to the negative comments, statements and thoughts in my brain, even if they weren't true, the ones that hindered my ability to step into my power and manifest my true desire. I know it's all about upbringing and conditioning but it should want to trust an opposite view that would help us towards our goals, instead of resisting and putting up walls to protect us from it. I get that when we're young, we're likely to accept any information offered, especially if from those we trust and we don't have the sophistication or discrimination to analyse or challenge it. I understand we get shaped by the feedback we receive from the world but why, if we ever made a mistake or caused an accident and got told we were stupid, clumsy or idiotic, did these comments register in our minds like solid facts, creating a negative sense of self during our development?

Usually, whether an affirmation is true or false, valid or invalid, it's secondary as far as the concerning principle of affirming. If we hear the negative thought, judgement or statement often enough, especially during our development, then the mind gradually accepts it as true, and in time, it becomes part of our reality. This deeply influences our perceptions, attitudes, moods and personalities.

When an affirmation produces a feeling, then it comes and goes as it pleases. You don't need to be told you're clumsy or stupid; it's absorbed sufficiently enough to make you act that way.

If a high proportion of thoughts that live inside our head are negative, then we get dragged down. This produces feelings of low self-worth and a critical view of ourselves and the world, which then saps us in our ability to achieve our goals. Positive, uplifting, and empowering affirmations are crucial if we are to create the healthy mental environment for a better life.

The reason our affirmations - whatever type they are - become beliefs is because of the repetition principle. We have to repeat something often enough for it to become an accepted member of your community of thoughts and feelings. Whether we root the belief in truth doesn't matter because unless we develop an immunity to negative influences, it's the repetition of the statement which ultimately leaves its neurological imprint on our minds.

Once this happens it hits the heart and trains it to put up walls, tighten DNA, close our ability to manifest things if our beliefs tell them it's dangerous for us and for this reason, it's our hearts that we must speak to when we're creating the affirmations. We may gain mental power from affirmations, but there are things to note before we override the heart. We are all a product of our circumstances, surroundings and upbringing, and the heart remembers the bad times as we mould into the unique humans we are today. What we think is usually what we believe, and it causes fear, our hearts will protect us. That doesn't mean we must stay fixed if the beliefs we have aren't working for us!

We just have to find affirmations our brains already find logical, so our hearts can't argue. And, unless it is a universal fact like the earth is round and you wish to believe it's flat, we can persuade our hearts to listen bit by bit.

If you were twenty stone and wanted to be a catwalk model, but knew the fashion gurus prefer cake-starved individuals, then you must think of this "major leap from the norm" in small doses until you get to a place where you can visualise walking down one. You could start off in a plus sized fashion show, affirming positive things about your body, your ability to walk with swagger, and your "won't be told no" attitude. Then imagine that sassy version of you on a catwalk. Add the feeling of how many women you will inspire, uplift and give confidence to as you lived your dream, and it will turn it into a spiritual goal too.

As we fire a "positive body" type neurone over and over, the neurone branches out more and more, pulsating, looking for nearby neurones to connect to it that will help support the growth of the new neurone and override the negative body image you have that destroys your confidence and limits you. Once it finds other thoughts of positive body images you've experienced, it strengthens the neural network of that new affirmation. Neural connectivity is important with affirmations but the heart must feel a sense of "okay, I can handle that minor fact, that's fine and won't hurt me" before we give it the whole shebang.

The thoughts that create deep-rooted feelings inside us are the ones that change our world and circumstances… or keep them the same. We can't always choose how we feel, yet in every moment, we can decide what to think and create a better emotion. Thinking positively (especially if believable) will create the electromagnetic energy our torus needs to produce a thoughtling, and hence the Resonation Realm that can carry our "ask" past the frequency fields.

I talk about the power of beliefs in my book Resonating System and how we need to rid ourselves of false ones that hinder us so we can adopt more beneficial ones that support us, which you should read to clear limiting beliefs. Affirmations are good for turning beliefs on their head or challenging them until we reach the new, beneficial belief.

For example, if you believe having too much money means others will somehow suffer, you can dispel it with an inner dialogue of, "that's like believing if I'm always well, others will be sick" and laughing. This not only beneficial challenges the belief, it relaxes the heart. Spiritual individuals programmed to believe they shouldn't want more, just need to get some spiritual sense. This is an expanding universe and we're here to assist this. The more we add value, the more we will have. There's enough for everyone, even if some people have nothing. Not one person has to suffer on this planet. If you have "plenty" (the improved word for too much), it doesn't take from people who have little. If you have "plenty", it will show others it's possible for them too. Plenty of money means you can even give some to others. How great would that be? This changes the first thought immediately. Others won't suffer if you have lots of money. The more money you have enables you to give to others who suffer.

An affirmation in advance to achieve this mindset (and hence into the Algorithmic Zone that guide us to the quickest path to getting plenty of money) would be "It's so great to give to others. I love being successful enough to be generous."

I like to say the affirmation, "I always get what I want, when there's no contradiction in my vibration" because it's true, and also reminds me to clear something in my system (and hence my vibration) if what I want isn't coming.

I also make sure I always state with true belief and a satisfied smile after the many times I've manifested exactly what I've wanted (meaning I've acted on the incline given to me by the Algorithmic Zone until I've brought my dream into my reality), is a slight adaptation to the "I always get what I want and truly believe" affirmation, and that's a simple "I always get what I want".

The reason I do this after the manifestation is to add more fuel to the statement. I then feel a sense of this as I put in my new "ask". When I notice the inclines and lightbulb moments coming to me quicker, it confirms the belief more and more.

Whatever I want, and know I can get without contradiction in my vibration, I will always get. But it has to be pure. It has to be aligned, both heart and mind, to boom the thoughtling into the particular Zone that will assist me. Another way to resonate with what you want is to ask yourself why you're already on your way to manifesting it. Mine, for example, would be, "why do I know I can easily lose weight" before I make the Resonation Realm that will allow me to imbue the "weight loss" power from the Vitality Zone. This helps me relax into the vibration of already having a metabolism that works well.

Answer 1: Because there are so many diets that I've not tried yet.

Answer 2: Because there are motivational speakers out there that I've not listened to that the Algorithmic Zone will guide me to.

Answer 3: Because I enjoy healthy foods.

With this, I claim the power to create instead of merely reacting to my physical circumstances and wanting to change it. We need this type of imaginary intervention to get our hearts to relax.

Reversing the effects of negative, doubtful thoughts is laborious, especially when old perceptions have been in place for years, but they can, with dedicated focus, diminish. One great way is to place the phrase 'I can' in front of your positive affirmation. We can later progress to 'I will' which is further up the affirmation spiral. 'I will' brings us closer to the positive state we need to achieve to tap into the Resonation Realm. In particular, the best prefix for any affirmation is 'I am'. The phrase shows the subconscious that you are what the declaration suggests. The repetition forms a new belief with an intrinsic positive feeling) but 'I am' causes the most resistance and doubt in the system, especially if you haven't worked up to it with logic.

To overcome the resistance, I write general questions starting with "I am", and then make myself fill in the gaps with facts that affirm it.

I have a great mind because…

I am fine because…

I am divine because…

I am worthy because…

I am strong because…

I am beautiful because…

I am loved because…

I am appreciated because…

I am relevant because…

I am unique because…

I am funny because…

I am successful because…

I deserve the thing I want because…

Make sure what you state feels right, so it resonates.

Also "I am" followed by an - ing verb, brings action into it, such as "I am becoming more patient" and it's a step below "I am". "I am becoming more patient" is easier to believe than "I am patient" for an impatient person. Ing verbs give us the impression of a continuous flow that we are entering slowly rather than a definite arrival that we must feel completely sure of.

Hence, why I teach that the affirmation has to resonate somewhat first.

There's no point looking in the mirror chanting "I am beautiful" if you've always been told you're pig ugly, and in fact you've entered many ugly contests and won. To reach a statement that is so far apart from your belief, you need to ask yourself things like:

Have I ever had a partner?

Did they think I was beautiful?

Did they look at me and treat me as if I was beautiful?

Am I kind, generous, have a good heart?

Do things make me beautiful on the inside?

Do people trust me?

Can people tell me anything?

Do I know I am gifted?

Do I enjoy my presence?

Am I fun to be around?

These things make a person beautiful! Never mind what body types the fashion gurus get to walk up and down catwalks, making society believe it's the consensus for beauty. It's in the beholder's eye, but you should see it too! If you look in the mirror like you're looking at a friend, what would you say to that friend? I bet, after describing all the wonderful qualities you have, you could say, without a doubt, you are beautiful.

There are sex symbols like Gérard Depardieu who,

to me, is what society would class as ugly. I mean, if he was in your local bar, sat with his head down, would as many women fancy him? Not a chance. He has something that no handsome face can beat — charisma! That is the X-factor of attraction. There's a hidden mystery in his eyes, a secret in his smile, intelligence in his charming accent; things any of us can portray. This proves that all humans, in all shapes and forms, are beautiful!

Maybe he has positive self-talk. Maybe his affirmations are powerful, heartfelt, and he strengthens them by how he feels, acts, and connects to the outside world! It's all about perspective.

Look at the model, Katie Piper. Having acid thrown in her face didn't change her identity.

To present shows with the honesty she does, despite what happened, gives other people the confidence to embrace who they are too. Watching her go through painful, reconstructive surgery and still act like herself makes me think of her as even more beautiful. Why? Because I respect her. I love her guts, her tenacity, her heart, and that she's given so many people inspiration. I don't see disfigurement; I see her soul!

Let me invite you to go to your mirror and look at yourself all miserable and slouched, stating that you're ugly. What do you see? Then sit straight, smile and wink at yourself, saying "you're so freaking beautiful," and watch your eyes light up. If you felt this confident all day, you would exude charm. As people respond well to your smiles, it will confirm that you are attractive, helping you believe you are beautiful.

So, if your affirmation is something that doesn't resonate, ask those questions. Analyse the facts and come up with ways your statement can resonate. Then say it, loud and proud!

You only need to find reasons you can believe the affirmation first before you state it. For example, if you're not already as successful as you want to be and you say "I am successful", and this doesn't produce a resonating feeling within you, focus on the statement and come up with reasons you're already successful.

If this isn't working, you must explore examples where you've felt the opposite of your affirmation. See where you planted the seed so you can uproot the whole plant. Perhaps it was your parents, or your culture, or the media that implanted a negative belief in your mind. As children, we sometimes propagate our parent's beliefs in order to please them. When we dig deep, we often find that our most prominent beliefs about ourselves are not even ours. This reason I started eating too much was because I couldn't scrape food off my plate when people across the globe were starving! Once I convinced myself that starving people didn't mean I had to be fat, I stopped eating when I was full. Sometimes when I scrape my plate, I get a pang of guilt from the memory, but I simply remind myself to put less on my plate next time.

There will be many ways in which you have been successful. Ever given up smoking or drinking? Already completed a university course towards your goal? Recount them. Once you affirm you are a person who can achieve success, you will achieve the thoughtling that gets you into the zone that will help guide you to the new success you want. Sometimes all it takes is perspective. We forget how many wonderful things we've already done or are doing and instead choose to focus on the failures. A reorientation towards the positive brings us halfway there because it gets us in! We then only need to take heed of the gifts we receive and we will soon achieve what we dream!

Affirmations are self-talk, and, whether internal or external, self-talk has a powerful influence over our self-worth and how we view ourselves and the world. We all have a self-talk going on in our heads as we go about our daily tasks. When we're in the shower and we see ourselves naked, we may have criticising thoughts. If someone ignores us, cheats on us, mistreats us in any way we may ask ourselves if we are enough. While eating, we may wonder how much weight we will gain. What responsive self-talk we use in our day-to-day mind chatter adds to the harmony or disharmony of our vibration.

Dr. Emoto says 'Everything is resonance.' His amazing water experiments literally show what the vibration of words can do.

If you've not heard of Dr. Masaru Emoto, or seen his water experiment, then I suggest you go to YouTube and watch him expose music, words, pictures and videos to water, and witness the waters' response, which is truly majestic.

Words like love, peace, joy, appreciation, happiness and gratitude,—ones that cause positive emotions — produce spectacular results. Words like hate, idiot, you make me sick, Adolph Hitler and demon — ones that cause negative emotions — create horrid and ugly shapes, or don't form into shapes at all. The particles either cave in or spin out, as if trying to escape the feeling the words induced.

Considering our bodies comprise at least 70% water, my advice is to speak to ourselves with love, appreciation and joy, or any words or acts which create high-frequency vibrations, the ones that only make you feel brilliant, natural, grateful, etc. Or, you can meditate and gain those great things without concentrating.

Since watching these experiments, I thank my water and speak to it lovingly before I drink it, and even swirl in reiki healing energy as I run my bath water, speaking words of appreciation before I step in. I even speak to the energy inside water based foods, thanking it for vitalising my body, which connects us to the Vitality Zone. Although I started with arthritis in my twenties, rheumatism and cartilage disease in my thirties, and fibromyalgia in my forties, I still have a gratitude journal and write something I appreciate about my body at the end of the evening. I also use ancient techniques for the pain.

Can the ancient tools I use cure ailments completely?

There may be a few well-trained monks who could get right into the heart of the Vitality Zone and draw from it a complete regeneration of healthy cells with meditation, mantra and positive thoughts enough to heal fully. For me, I don't have as many bouts of pain (and therefore spend more time in remission) as others who suffer from the same autoimmune diseases as myself. I try to stay extremely grateful for that, but I get miffed by it sometimes (which is only natural for a northerner who growls internally when things go wrong), especially when my body doesn't work. Also, my awareness of being a spirit in skin gives me the "human" sense to know at all times that my body is just a mortal avatar that is debilitating in its own way, before I return to my realm where no pain exists.

Unlike what Law of Attraction would have us believe, I know we don't always cause unpleasant situations. Sometimes outside forces cause things to happen. This mindset keeps me from acting like a victim. We came to experience the world, warts and all. We knew that we'd grow, learn or find some understanding for others we didn't have before, add value where we can, and take back how we've been of service. The pain of my body serves to remind me I'm running out of time, my biological avatar-clock will not tick forever, and that I must hurry to make the creative work I wish to leave for this purpose, to stay on track with my endeavour.

I'm also aware of what we can cause to our bodies with our negativity. When our heart suffers too many consistent negative emotions caused by our negative self-talk, it's not only our ability to boom that we must concern ourselves with. Because our hearts shrivel and lock in the low vibrational energy, emotions can harm us physically too, if the thoughts that cause them are persistent.

The water swirling inside our bodies acts like a mirror to our interiors. Our thoughts and feelings create a positive or negative pattern inside the water and will stay that way, perpetuating that feeling until we change the pattern or simply let it go. If we don't change or clear the negative code that water holds, it can cause health problems. Your reticular activating system will always spring into action and find you more of the things you're focused upon, so change your focus on whatever tool is best and start changing the code. A well trained RAS will allow you to search for ways you can categorically state that you are healthy, successful... or anything else you'd prefer to be, do or have in your life.

The key is to focus on resonating with your statements. Feel as if what you want is with you now with pure love so you are vibrating with the positive emotion it causes, which speeds up your efforts in bringing the thing you desire into its full manifestation. It's a bit like sympathetic resonance in the sense that the higher realms vibrate on an emotional level that's divine and full of love and peace. (I talk more about this in my book, Resonating Mantras: Make The Universe Dance To Your Chant.) Basically, you hit a key on one piano, and the same note on a nearby piano will chime. When you pluck a string on one guitar, another close by will start vibrating that same string.

When you think of your desire without fear, just the beautifulness of having it in your life, living exactly the way you intended on living when you came to this planet, you then vibrate on a purer, more spiritual, higher dimensional level. It's not that you become a magnet to the people, things and circumstances (they can't suddenly be drawn to you like they are magnetic or have no free will of their own now you've made yourself vibe on their level), it's that you're now vibrating without contradiction. If there is no fear within you of having it, and your persona and psyche agree, your energy will reverberate at a level that matches the Prime Mystical Zones.

When you do this, you will receive the gifts from them that give us the inclines and lightbulb moments we take heed of to succeed with speed... because we're unlikely to ignore them, second guess them or procrastinate in this mode because we're already fine with it.

The emotion we create has to feel so natural to you it would feel stranger not having it.

Check your self talk! Unresolved, unconscious, energy blockages must go. It's important to dedicate some time to uncorking blocked avenues, otherwise the affirmations have no clear alleyways to flow through and do their work, no matter how positive and powerful they are!

It's your responsibility to keep yourself in a great state. If you're empty, fill yourself up with light and love. Feel your inner being and sense your true identity. You are a spiritual being, having a human experience. Feel that and learn how to express it. Don't allow your mind to stop at surface level or you may manifest things only to realise that you didn't truly want them, and what you actually needed was something even deeper. There is a meaningful process involved in truly seeing what motivates us to want what we want (and thus say affirmations to get them).

Ask for the real thing, instead of the "how" of it.

THE RESONATING AFFIRMATIONS

*A*re my "Resonating Affirmations" just something we repeat to ourselves consistently, which is also in line with what we trust and already somewhat believe, then?

Almost.

I mean, the word "resonant" shows the affirmation must be deep and clear within your vibration, so if you can find evidence to sustain the statement that is difficult for your mind to argue with then it's a Resonating Affirmation. But this resonance applies to any affirming you're doing, whether it is good or bad. If you believe what you think, that belief (whether true or false) will get you into the zones or keep you out of them. Resonance is akin to believing, and beliefs gain more momentum. Over time, they become dominant and morph into something that feels real. To wire in a new beneficial belief purposefully to override the old limiting one, choose things that already seem right to the logical part of your brain and feel right to the intelligence inside your heart. Or, in extreme cases, the awareness of your higher subconscious (if your lower mind is biassed) and the truth inside your soul (if your heart won't give up its protection enough to release the feeling of fear that shuts you down).

Trust is the key here. You can't reprogram the brain with false beliefs. You actually have to believe them enough to banish the fear or at least relax the heart enough with the reasoning you give it that any consequence to come out of gaining the desire you crave will be nothing it can't handle. Be happy to take on the perceived negative side to something as a part of the thing that will bring you the much wanted benefits, acting like it will be worth it.

In particular, plant new seeds in your brain that will sprout into things that benefit you. The best affirmations are those you create for yourself and that resonate with you enough in the beginning that you can already believe in them. You may find generic affirmations that almost everyone should be able to resonate with, but truths of your own will eliminate your deficiencies.

I can say and believe that, no matter what I'm

going through, whether through my actions or just because unwanted stuff simply happens, the Prime Mystical Zones know what's preferable for me and will direct me to all I want when I trust that good always comes out of bad. It's a great feeling to just "give it up to the powers above". To trust in the divine intelligence and know that the Zones are working the quickest path to your dreams out for you makes the feel-good factor last longer. Whether an unforeseen circumstance is because of my thoughtlings, prompting me to analyse why I'm perpetuating them and doing something about them, or whether I realise it was just something that happened, I only have to set about creating a new affirmation to suit what I now wish to develop and trust I will be led to it.

You can trust in the Zones and in yourself. Think about it, haven't you already successfully gotten through everything life has dished out to you? Sometimes I see that a first perceived "bad" situation led me to the thing I wanted. I believe good sometimes comes out of bad, especially so if we look for a positive outcome hidden within it. When this happens, I simply thank the universe for my positive perspective and blessing in disguise. If we tell the Algorithmic Zone we can do this, it may bring us what we want in faster ways. I don't mean welcome horrible things in, we're not asking for things that hurt us mentally, physically or emotionally; just impartial, insignificant things others may deem as bad, yet the universe knows won't be a problem to us. This doesn't mean you if you're tough enough and want money you'll end up in a car crash so you get the compensation. Even if that idea sounds appealing and exciting to you, the Algorithmic Zone wouldn't find this quick. They'd have to wait until they found some murderous drunk driver who's higher self needs someone to take their licence from them before they kill an innocent child (or some other match) before they sent the incline for them to step on the gas or let go of the wheel right behind you.

The "idea" of making someone crash into you from behind wouldn't have come from the Algorithmic Zone, neither. If you had an idea like that, then it came from your lower persona. Deliberately causing a crash with an innocent driver is not something spiritual people would do, no matter how desperate for money!

The zones only send ideas or purposely line us up with things they know we can brush off, laugh about and thank, so you don't have to fear disasters. I mean simple things that others may find a big deal, but not you. One example of this was when my car got stolen. Which allowed me to share my mum's car, saving me the money on insurance I was moaning about when wondering how I could save money each month. How it gave the person who stole cars the incline to steal mine instead of someone else's who'd be more upset is down to their "ask". I mean, serendipity could have played a part as coincidences happen more often than we give them credit for. What I know is the Zone wouldn't direct a thief to my car unless he was already questioning which car to steel and asking it to guide him to one that would cause the least grief to someone for them to direct them to my car.

My point being, through every test we've had on this planet, the Algorithmic Zone knows that we have either come through and succeeded, or failed and learned. It also knows what would hurt our hearts and would never risk guiding us to that. It's not like we need to do anything about the inclines and lightbulb moments we receive from them, anyway. We can simply choose not to act on what we receive. You should trust yourself no matter what system you believe in. We all have free will and choice. Choosing to take control of the thoughts and feelings inside the machine your soul assimilated in gives you the advantage, though.

Thoughts need opinions about them, opinions create feelings about the thought, and feelings create an open or closed fear or trust emotion in the heart. We need to trust the Prime Mystical Zones will never harm us or bring us the crap we curse the universe, God, Law of Attraction and karma for. The Zones work for us always, not against us. We can only become more confident, successful humans when we tap into them, shifting that underlying fear further and further away so it never feels like shrinking or tightening again.

Most people doubt their beliefs and believe their doubts, both of which are the protection mechanism inside our system to protect us from danger, but when we don't want or need the protection, we must get rid of it. The first process in creating a Resonating Affirmation is to ask if the belief you're trying to change is more of a conviction. Convictions are stronger than beliefs and therefore harder to remove. The wires are more ground in. Like when we try to remove strict religious beliefs to a more spiritual practice but you feel somehow bad that you've stopped worshiping the man in the sky version of God because of the fear of Him sending us to hell, even though your logic doesn't resonate with the notion that a divine, loving being with infinite understanding would do such a thing.

Thankfully, asking questions will help loosen the wires of conviction. The way we do this is by asking both our persona and psyche questions. This way we can wobble the wires.

1. Is what you fear true universally, or is the fear just in your heart because of your conditioning?

2. Would others who truly know you think it was logical for you to fear this?

3. What would you say to yourself if this was the belief of your best friend (or person you truly wish well).

4. If it's true to your personified perspective, what does your more intelligent self, deep within your gut and subconscious, think of this belief? Breathe this higher perspective up into your heart and mind so it will no longer stifle you.

5. Is it true to source? Wouldn't the infinite, divine IT think you had a duty to make the most of your gifts in the limited time you have got in this form?

Sometimes our hearts know when we're tricking them and will shut down if in doubt. But there's nothing scary about asking a simple question. Even if we don't like the answer or don't wish to go for the answer because of new fears that may spring to life inside the heart (because of it wanting to protect us from its perceived danger), the heart will still open itself to receive answers as it knows it remains in control of whether to open or close to your acting upon that answer. Our hearts will always welcome in knowledge as it would rather not be in a constant state of fear and it knows more knowledge can reduce the fear, if it makes sense. To the heart, asking questions is akin to finding out how to reduce your fear, so you 're actually doing something it wants, which is to feel happy and safe. This is easier than asking for something despite the heart, i.e. going for a desire it fears regardless of the fear.

We can use questions like stepping stones towards the big goal so it's not so much of a scary change. Try to find ones which you know have logical answers (as in fears you know others don't worry about), and keep digging deeper into the core of your blockage. I used this process when I went from writing songs for unsigned bands to joining one as a backing singer. My heart allowed this bridge because I convinced it I could hide behind the lead vocalist, allowing me to get used to singing on stage which weaned me to screaming out solo parts like I was one of Pink Floyd's backing singers for the great gig in the sky!

It was only after a random guy grabbed me after a gig and said "shit hot, that vocal of yours" that realised I'd weaned my heart in with baby steps. I could've cried "thanks" because of my soul zooming around my entire body in delight. My heart gave out the most wonderful sense of release in that moment that it surprised me I didn't knock the guy over with the blast of light, booming out the years of fear.

If ever my confidence gets knocked, I have a set of "reminder" type Resonating Affirmations I like to repeat to. I feel these affirmations serve me the most, no matter what I'm going through, to remind me of who I truly am! I root them in things I can somewhat believe after much rational thought or from "acting like I am my best friend" when creating them, of course so they resonate with my persona and psyche.

They are:

I am loving!

I am kind!

I am trustworthy!

I am helpful!

I am caring!

I am creative!

I am funny!

I am strong!

I am humble!

I have a good heart!

I am a good listener!

I have good intentions!

I have a great mind!

I have super kids who love me!

I am fantastic at manifesting!

I know I deserve success!

I have lots of resourceful means around me and flowing to me at all times!

I am liked by many and loved by the people who matter most to me!

I have lots of people around me who love and care for me and my wellbeing!

I have done many things I'm proud of, and this has helps me to know I can do anything I put my mind to!

I always get what I want and honestly believe I will get!

I know my body, mind, and genetic make-up remembers how to be my ideal weight, and I know I can quickly lose weight and keep it off forever if I put my mind to this!

I am getting a leaner and fitter mindset each day. I'm resonating with healthy foods now. I'm enjoying eating healthy!

Each day, I am more confident in knowing I can handle all aspects of my life.

I always handle situations in the present moment with ease - therefore, no matter what the future brings, I will be okay!

I trust myself entirely to handle any situation!

I can turn whatever I perceive to be terrible that

comes my way into something wonderful and positive!

The universe knows what's best for me and plots to bring me what I need, want, and desire!

And that's just a few!

With each of these "reaffirming" Resonating Affirmations, I make sure I avoid the preface "I will" or "I want to" because I this only gives me a feeling of I "one day will" and the fact that I "want to", not that I actually can or am. If you only communicate that you will or you want to, the vibration will remain in the lower dimensions where we only want and intend to but never do because they have a vibration of lack in them. We need the "higher feeling of love and trust" it takes to push past the lower frequencies. If you say I *can* or better still I *am*, your vibration will reach higher dimensions.

Reread them and see if you can resonate with them. Ask yourself "am I loving?" and "in what ways do I know this to be true?" If any of them sound like something you can resonate with, then keep them. Tweak some if necessary. Grab a pen and some blank, beautiful card and write some truths about yourself around what you wish to manifest.

If you find it difficult at first to find great things about yourself, think what your friends would say your best qualities are. Write each one after the words, "I am" (whatever it is), even if I add "according to my best friend… and I can believe her because I trust her" to the end. Starting them with "I have", "I always", or "I know" helps too.

"I am" is also powerful in its own right, as this is said to invoke the light of God. If said alone on repeat, it will awaken your soul, therefore, it is one of the most powerful mindset shifting, spirit lifting affirmations you can begin your new beneficial affirmation with. I like to do some easy ones with universal truths before I put in the harder beliefs. For example…

I AM… able to think with logic, and reason and see situations impartially

I AM… understanding that opportunities for everyone are also for me

Sometimes I say the "I am" part as "Ah Yam", which is a powerful seed syllable for healing and aligning the heart chakra.

Ah yam… attractive

Ah yam… successful

Ah yam… fit, healthy, and strong

Ah yam… a brave soul in control

If none of them make you feel like a warrior when you say them (like they should) it means they don't quite resonate enough yet to empower you. If you notice the dichotomy, just wobble the wires for now with something like…

Ah yam… attractive (to my perfect mate)

Ah yam… successful (in so many things)

Ah yam… becoming fit and strong as I think more healthy

Ah yam… able to teach my heart that it has nothing to fear, and that I don't need protecting from the things my mind conjures up.

Ah Yam… able to deem negative situations as a simple consequence that comes with successful beings.

Tony Robbins says that when he does affirmations, he declares the words in such a way that he's shouting his head off at himself so they become more of an incantation. He will yell, "I will show my body who's boss of it. I am the driving force of this ship, the master of my emotions". I mean, I would sit up and listen if the giant Tony Robbins was screaming into my soul, even if I was Tony Robbins! You don't mess with a powerhouse like that, even if your whole physiology wanted to do nothing but procrastinate when heading towards a goal, or you're craving to eat crap because you've been restricting yourself, your soul would wake up and drive your ship if you yelled loud enough at it. Tony shouts at himself so powerful, he's actually chanting his words like they are a magic spell, which is one reason the incantations overcome whatever it is he's shouting at himself to overcome.

Just a brief note here to those who find blowing their own trumpet and trying to feel empowered somewhat icky. If you're British, like me, you may find shouting in this manner a bit off-putting but that's only because of the "collective consciousness" of our culture where most of us believe it is obnoxious to "brag about ourselves". So we must make it clear to ourselves that we are not doing this so we can walk down the street with our noses above the crowds, lording it over the masses; this is a very private ritual we must undertake to sort out our damaged, limiting, crap-filled brains and hearts so we can be who we came to this planet to be. It's helping us return to the innocent, lovely, humble version of ourselves that we were before any nonsense (collective consciousness or not) took over the truth we knew in our souls.

We will only act like proud, brilliant nutters in front of ourselves so make sure you do this with the full oomph it requires. The secret can remain between the two of you; psyche and persona. The rest of the population only has to witness the effects the incantations have on you (i.e. your confidence and success), which all your friends will love to see. Every human living as their true self wants to see other souls achieve the things they want to achieve, especially when they do so with their full heart and soul, no matter what their personas may think. That's why we tear up when people win talent shows.

Incantations are like spiritual chant because of the power of rhythm and sound. You can learn how chanting naturally uplifts the spirit in my book Resonating Mantras, make the universe dance to your chant but, simply, incantations make our affirmations become more potent. Not only do the tones uplift the spirit, just like a song, chanting gives a certain reverberation to the words that make the Resonation Realm we're creating buzz.

This led me to the idea of using rhyme, especially when creating my most powerful Resonating Affirmations. That's the secret to my ultimate Resonating Affirmations; they must not only be something we repeat to ourselves consistently, which is also in line with what we trust and already somewhat believe, but also rhyme! Rhyming adds the last bit of magic to the formula.

Why do rhymes have magical power?

The jolly sounds we create when we sing these types of rhythmic affirmations raise our vibration, which means we are more likely to match the vibrational waves that pervade the higher dimensions. The divine dance is full of joyful tones and our creation of them will find their match (as sympathetic resonance proves). If we sing our affirmations, we automatically lift our spirits into the feeling place of the Prime Mystical Zones. Making them silly, jolly or childlike also takes the "trying to resonate with something deep and important" aspect out of them, eliminating the desperate urgency mode we can sometimes include when we really want something. Singing important words this lightly and care free automatically makes us feel giddy and puts us in a place of excited fun, instead of a "this doesn't feel like me" place.

Things that stick inside our minds more than anything are things that are taught well, things that are stimulating, or things we are interested in. The mind comes alive when it's intrigued. Words that resonate with us uniquely, like particular little phrases, famous quotes by great minds, fables and anecdotes, stimulate our hearts too, that's why we find them easier to listen to and remember.

We have used rhyming words for centuries to conjure glorious feelings and powers, especially in a magical spells, and it's for a good reason. They're easy to remember. The chanting style promotes a ritualistic feel, hence giving us the true awe-filled mystical feeling that enhances emotions, giving them inherent power. Rhyming will no doubt speed up the power of your Resonating Affirmation because there's been a particular subtle allurement to poems that connect to our souls (which are naturally creative) so they help stimulate the mind. We connect to and appreciate them. They provoke our thoughts. Our psyche wakes up and our persona listens up. When things ring true to us too, we will never forget what they said.

It, therefore, makes sense that if we can create affirmations (or use ones we resonate with) in this way, the brain and heart will tune into the mystical Zones because they are free to produce better thoughtlings or at least clear the crap in our systems that hinders our ability to create them.

Can you resonate with this poem?

I am a child of the universe

Light and love live inside of me

I can think and feel in ways

that create my preferred reality

Not only is it correct, but because it rhymes, it creates a sense of ritual, a feeling that what you're saying has some inherent power to it. Short poems like this are easy to put together. Here's one I made for myself when I want to lose weight...

My body is vibration

it remembers being slim

I don't have to eat so differently
or even go to the gym
I only have to resonate
with the foods I eat
just make better choices
that I know benefit me
I can be healthy minded
fill myself with vitality
Because I'm made of energy
That's lightweight and free
I can continue till I'm bored
of this heavier version of me
then decide to grow a pair
And work for my body.

You can use them too if they fully resonate with you or simply adapt them to suit your own specific needs so they still rhyme at the end. When you repeat your Resonating Affirmations in this rhyming, jolly mantra style enough times, your RAS will align with the feelings produced. Instead of just empty words, you are creating "resonating words" and also have natural power in them to lift your spirit to boot. You will feel genuinely magic, as what you're chanting appears in your life (due to you staying in tune with the data that comes back and you act upon until you manifest it, of course; not that it just appears like magic).

Using the power of rhyme with persistence and patience will ensure any opposition left in your vibration will eventually evaporate, and in its place will emerge a fertile mind, one that's able to produce thoughtlings that are healthy and empowering. If you feed your mind with a diet of positive, uplifting thoughts with the power of rhyme, you will brilliantly penetrate your Resonation Realm with your "ask" of the Zones and hence be able to experience the magic of the Resonating Affirmation right away (as the gifts this will allow you to imbue, invoke or download enters your system and starts giving you lightbulb moments and gut inclines right away).

Realise for this act to have lasting and irreversible effects in your life, it needs to be a regular feature of your existence. With the power of rhyme, the affirmations penetrate deeper into the complex vibrations of the mind, cultivating a stronger alignment. Before long, you will have more time and abundance, and your relationships will transform — in short, you'll become a happier, more positive person. Even your physical health will improve. Things will happen in your life that you never thought possible, and even difficult people will start to reflect your positive vibrations.

I'm hoping Resonating Affirmations resonate with you as they do for me and, therefore, work faster than any other affirmations you've tried when attempting to undo the negative program/ set of beliefs we know we must rid ourselves of. I also hope you will remember them quickly enough so you can quote them any time a negative person tries to bring you back down to their level. You should be able to relay something with a huge, satisfied smile on your face and, because you'll say it with kindness and mean well, it will intrigue them. Even if they don't believe in them, they'll watch you for the hope of proof and, once your life changes, they'll not only have it, they will ask you how on Earth everything always goes well for you.

That's when you can say without doubt: there is real magic in this universe and my heart and mind can connect to it. I can therefore create the life I want with the help I get from its gifts!

—THE 7 SPIRIT LIFTING, MINDSET
SHIFTING, RESONATING
AFFIRMATIONS ON THE PLANET—

My 7 spirit lifting, mindset shifting, Resonating Affirmations are rhyming affirmations that nobody's soul
or logic can disagree with when considered, therefore
they automatically soften the heart, allowing you to
conjure the joyful, worthy, and relaxed emotions you
need to boom your intent into the Zone that will
support it, which also allows your brains to form the
new beneficial belief that all things are possible.

Repeated enough times (using a jolly or dramatic
tone), they wobble away all old neurological wires in
the brain that cause negative self-talk and limiting
beliefs and allow us to replace them with a new positive mindset that help us gain beneficial beliefs that
create the thoughtlings we need to tap into the Zones
that gift us the means to our dreams. With the gifts we

receive, we can work towards our goals with ease and keep reinforcing the new belief.

Before you chant, incant or declare my 7 powerful Resonating Affirmations, take a moment to close your eyes and breathe in the truth of who and what you truly are, so the eternal psyche version of you lifts into your consciousness so you can feel it more than the biological persona you have crafted in this temporary, biased form. That way, they'll resonate with the two of you as one whole.

Also, voice them in a rhythmic, melodic, jolly way or prepare yourself to think of them in that manner, if you're not alone. You can also listen to them with the MP3 I give away when you sign up to my email list. You can sign up and download this MP3 (if you haven't already) on my website: spiritualjoye.com. The accompanying music I've made to support the 7 of them matches the divine sounds that the higher dimensions use. I use binaural beets to achieve this, and also chant the ancient, powerful OM AH HU mantras over the top to give the extra reverberated power to push your desire past the frequency fields, which gives your specific "ask" (that you will make at the end of the last RA) the extra push it needs to reach the correct Mystical Zone you need.

DIVINITY IN ME

My potential is abundant;
I am as gifted as anyone else,
Because I am a divine spirit
Aware of my personified self

I know that I am able
to get what I desire,
I can do or be or have
anything I require

My definition of what the world is,
is what my world bias will seem,
So I can create a real difference
when I simply change my belief.

ADORE

If I focus on it entirely;
whatever it is I desire,
And adore it before I've secured it,
I'll soon have what I require

The thoughtlings I generate within
Will get me into the zones
That gift me the means to my dreams
that I can then hone

They come in the form of healings
Of ideas and inspiration
But mostly it's the gut inclines
I follow til manifestation

EASE

I can focus on more positive things
at any time I please,
Therefore, I can work through struggle
And create a sense of ease.

Emotions are my signals,
an inner knowing that holds the key,
Once I create a feeling of love,
I boom out the intent in me

The Mystical zones are ready
to gift me what I need,
Especially when my heart is happy
And my brain fully believe.

QUESTION

I question whether it's possible,
And if so welcome it in,
If I'm fearless of it coming to me,
My Resonation Realm will begin

To enter the mystical zones
That gift me the powers I need
so I can have what I truly desire
And what my soul can achieve

It's as easy as flicking a switch,
as gentle as a cool summer breeze,
To be in alignment with all I need
is to be loving, joyful, and free.

WOBBLE THE WIRES

We're a product of our circumstances
And our upbringing,
Both of which contribute
To what we choose to believe

Thankfully, our brains are wired
In ways that can be undone
We just have to challenge the limiting mind
That programs our whole system

We can wobble the wires
Lay down the new foundation
To install new beneficial beliefs
That support what we wish to become

SPIRIT OF IT

I know more than the version
I have crafted in this experience
This personified and conditioned part
That sometimes makes no sense

The truth is deep inside of me
I can perceive IT right now
I just ask my soul a question
And the answer will come out

In an open or closed feeling
That shows me a yes or a no
A sense of ease or tightening
Will give me all IT knows

TUNE

My brain and heart can be miles apart
When perusing my most desired goals,
But I can make sure they are aligned
With the true intent of my soul

The Resonation Realm that surrounds me
Holds energy which can't be seen,
But With my thoughtlings it can tune in
To the zones so I can receive.

I can do this with peace and pure love,
Or by having joyous fun.
I then enter the higher dimensions
When I raise my vibration,

I AM

I AM is what the almighty said
when IT first boomed out to create
Divide and design is what the sound did
Laying out the dimensions of space

Each layer down from this source
breathes into all time and matter
As the divine dance of particles,
Continue to scatter

I am made of vibration
And an energy that's supreme,
I am an extension of love,
a creative being.

～

Now you can take another breath and visualise having the thing you wish to manifest, feel how great it feels, how better off you are, and conjure a feeling of gratefulness or any time of loving or relaxed feeling and repeat…

I think of what I want, need, or desire
and perceive unity to it in my soul,
For my intent will add value to
the universe as a whole…

Keep repeating this until you feel as if you already have the thing you want, need or desire, or that you intend to make happen has happened, and it's all gone well.

End with…

Each layer down from this source
breathes into all time and matter
As the divine dance of particles,
Continue to scatter
I am made of vibration
And an energy that's supreme,
I am an extension of love,

a creative being.

I wish you the best of luck in all you do and hope you will believe in yourself enough to step into your power and become the genuine spirit in skin you came to this planet to be.

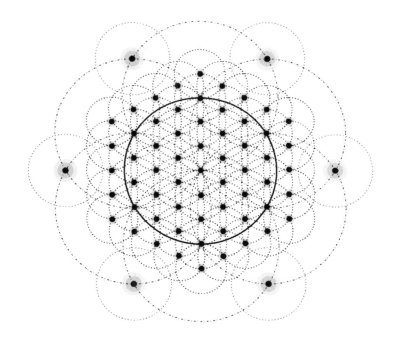

NOTE FROM THE AUTHOR

Thank you for purchasing Resonating Affirmations. I wrote it so we can remain in a high vibration, stay focused on the right feelings, and thus be better at using our innate powers.

I hope this tool has been as useful to you, that it's allows you to eliminate the stress and anxiety that everyday life has upon us and therefore you enter the Resonation Realm more often.

I hope the Resonating Affirmations align with your heart and mind and therefore help you on your way. I know the more you affirm your preferred thoughts and open your heart, the faster you will become at manifesting all you want in your life.

~

If you enjoyed this book, then you may like my other books in the Resonation Realm series. Resonating System: What To Perceive So You Can Achieve is a book that will give you the "skills" you need to gain access to the three mystical zones with ease. Resonating Meditations: Attract Something While You Do Nothing, and Resonating Mantras: Make The Universe Dance To Your Chant, are the two other "tools" you need to succeed, alongside this book. The reprogramming and spiritual sense that Resonating System gives, together with the three tools, will allow you entry into the Mystical Zones on autopilot, which will turn you into a supermundane force, manifesting all you want, need and desire.

If you are interested to go deeper with my tools, there are lots of free resources on my website you can benefit from too, including some of my Resonating Meditations and Resonating Mantras. The reason I give a lot away is so everyone can benefit, and hoping once you see the free tools and skills are of immense benefit, you may like to purchase the more in-depth, premium Resonating MP3s or go deeper with a course at a later date. I have lots more valuable services and products on my website for people who wish to learn more.

~

And, if you haven't got them already, don't forget to grab your gifts!

My Resonating Affirmations MP3 has my powerful "Declarations Required To Manifest Your Desires", and will resonate with what your soul already believes, which helps you rid yourself of limiting beliefs and replace them with the new beneficial truths that bring you into full alignment with universal forces. Also, the unique music has specific frequencies, designed to open your heart, and release the tight strands of your DNA, hence helping you boom into the Mystical Zones.

There's also a Resonating Affirmations for Love MP3 and a Resonating Affirmations for Money MP3 and a twice yearly gift of something I sell on my website. I will class you as a friend once you are on my Resonation Realm Readers list and only wish to share with you all the best ways we can vibrate higher so I can guide us to all we want in life with ease. And I will always remain honoured and respectful of your privacy while sharing this journey with you.

Hopefully, this book has awakened something inside you to dispel those deep fears, allowing the lotus flower to open inside your heart, freeing whatever debris has gathered inside so that you can see results.

I hope you find everything you want and more, and hope you're just as happy even if they don't come... therefore they will. I hope you strive to be mindful at all times and live in the now as often as possible.

I would love to spread the Resonation Realm message around the world, even hold Resonation Realm retreats where all fans and advocates could meet all up and send out positivity signals into the aether, so we can heal the world and get back the same love we put in. I'd love these retreats to be in beautiful locations all over the world, with like-minded people who want to embrace meditation, mantra, Reiki, yoga, gong baths, art, poetry, dance, and in the evening we could sing songs by a campfire under the stars, or have silent time, where we can share ethical, healthy (resonating) foods and discussions, and where, after we'd finished, we would leave with a higher vibration and radiating positivity, wherever we went — like it was infectious.

I believe if just 1% of the population attended these events, and sent light and love into the universe, a spiritual shift would occur on the entire planet. (I explain more about the Mashurachi effect in my book *Resonating Meditations; Attract Something While You do Nothing*.) I believe, if everyone knew how to use their power, then our planet could heal disease and it would be a more beautiful realm to experience. If you would like to help these places manifest in our world, there's a donation page on my website. All those who donate will have their name carved into a Reiki imbued art wall at each centre.

If you can't help via a donation right now, but enjoyed the book and would like to help in a way that is free to you but valuable to me, I would appreciate you leaving me a review. Some people won't buy a book without validation from others so your review will not only help spread the love and light so that others may find the information, but also help me as an author, which will help all I envision to come into fruition. My success will enable me to give to more to the charity "Mind" too, so you will contribute towards making a happier, healthier, and more positive planet for us all.

I wish you the best health, spiritual growth and happiness this life could bring and beyond. I wish you much abundance, peace and love and much spiritual growth.

Blessings, Rinzen x

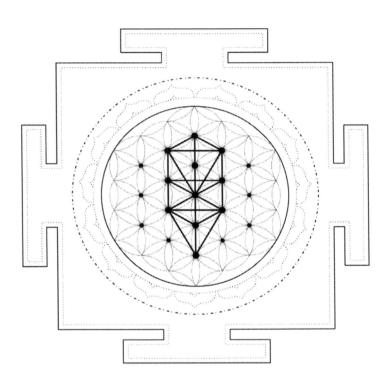

NAMASTE

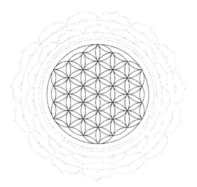

Printed in Great Britain
by Amazon